Healthy Teeth
For Life

Healthy Teeth For Life

by

Dianne Davis Gillentine

1stBooks - rev. 03/16/00

Healthy Teeth For Life gives to every man, woman and parent, help in simple effective ways to avoid pain to teeth and gums, with easy at-home cleaning of teeth and exercises of gums. This is to help everyone save money on dental treatments. It will also give insight on tips to stop sensitive teeth, dry mouth, ulcers and TMJ (temporomandibulat join) Syndrome. It also gives aids for more effective cleaning.

Dedication

I am indebted to my parents, Oliver Thurston Davis and Sarah Alene Sparkman, who, thirty years ago, gave me the support and encouragement I needed to continue my education to become a dental hygienist.

Forward

These are helpful exercises and ideals of dental care to keep teeth and gums healthy for a lifetime.

Cover art provided by Joe Brinkman Dental Art.

Exercise For Healthy Gums and Teeth

Care of teeth and gums is like exercising. If you only brush for a few seconds each time - that is not enough exercise. Good daily dental care is the same as exercise for the heart, arms, and legs, and other parts of the body. The teeth must be kept clean and free of plaque and food. To achieve this healthy dental state, it takes daily exercise and a commitment to want to keep your mouth disease free.

Teeth give the face its shape and form, help in the clear pro-nunciation of different sounds, and aid in chewing and digesting food.

Just as daily exercise and a commitment keep the heart and body healthy, so do good daily dental care and, a commitment keep the teeth clean of plaque and food and free of disease. It also keeps the gums firm, free of bleeding and drainage, and tight to the teeth.

Flossing

The most important part of our daily regiment is FLOSSING! Three times a day is recommended. Flossing removes the plaque and food particles that accumulate in the little hidden corners and crevices that we're unaware of. These particles, if left to decay, will produce a gas and an acid that will eat slowly at the bone around the teeth.

FLOSSING CORRECTLY

First, find a floss that you like and one that will slip gently and easily between your teeth. Johnson and Johnson's or Glide by Gore are highly recommended. Using ten to twelve inches of floss, wrap it around each index finger keeping only a small space between fingers. With your thumb, put floss between teeth at an angle. Curve the floss around each tooth, and go down under the tissue. Remove the floss at an angle and continue to floss all your teeth using this same method.

*Floss is the
heart of home care.*

NEVER let twenty-four hours go by without flossing.

After you have flossed, rub the tissue with clean fingers to exercise and keep gums firmer.

Floss holders are available for people with large hands or whose fingers lack the dexterity needed to floss.

Bridgework should be flossed with the aid of floss threaders or super floss each time you brush.

BRUSHING

Select a brush with a soft head that is small enough to permit access to all the surfaces of all the teeth and one that fits well in your mouth. Start with a fluoride and tartar-control toothpaste you like.

Rinse hot water over your brush before brushing to soften bristles.

Brush the chewing surface first; this helps to prevent gum re-cession. The average person usually applies too much pressure with the first four strokes of brushing. This causes abrasion at the gum line when the sides are brushed first.

Brush teeth in the direction they grow. Start at the front of the mouth and brush to the back reaching both teeth and gums.

To remove food and plaque, brush within fifteen minutes of eating, and floss well after each meal.

Healthy teeth
make a smile.

Once a day, after brushing with toothpaste, rinse with an anti-septic rinse such as Listerine for thirty seconds. If the rinse burns or is unpleasant, put some in a cup, dip your brush in it, and then brush.

Rub the tissue thirty seconds to one minute every day.

Brushing too harshly, back and forth or sideways, can make the gums recede and erode the enamel causing sensitivity to cold, sweets, pressure, temperatures, and the toothbrush.

Right-handed people brush longer on the left side. The right side often has softer gums and heavier plaque on individuals that are right-handed. The left side will often have greater abrasion at the gum line from brushing too hard and from brushing incorrectly.

Brush your teeth within minutes after eating for no one eats snacks as often when teeth are clean. This also helps you watch your waistline.

The new technology in electric brushes is a good method for removing plaque and reducing gingivitis. These brushes are helpful to the handicapped and elderly who may have trouble brushing.

Nighttime brushing is the most important for cleaning teeth.

Always brush gently and carefully.

Toothbrushes stay damp and collect food particles making the brush a carrier of bacteria. Pouring Listerine over the brush helps keep the bacteria under control.

If your toothbrush bristles become flattened out to the side of the head of the brush, you're brushing too hard.

Use Soft Brush.

Store your toothbrush, covered, in a drawer or cabinet out of the way of dust and water.

A toothbrush should be replaced at least every three months. If it becomes frayed or bent or you have a contagious illness, it should be replaced at that time.

FLUORIDE

Fluoride, the most effective anticavity agent available, is an essential element that hardens tooth enamel making the teeth stronger and more resistant to tooth decay.

Water with fluoride helps greatly to reduce cavities. Most bottled water contains low levels of cavity fighting fluoride.

Use toothpaste with fluoride to help reduce tooth decay.

Babies over six months old who are breastfed exclusively, children who drink only bottled water, or children who live in communities without a fluoridated water supply should have fluoride supplements.

Choose your home water purification system carefully as some systems destroy the fluoride in water.

RINSES

Pre-rinses make your mouth taste better, your breath smell good, your teeth smooth, as well as soften plaque.

Rinse with a germ-fighting mouth rinse daily to help control plaque formations.

Germ-fighting mouth rinses add protectives that kill plaque bacteria that the brush and floss cannot. An antiseptic mouth

"Ignore Your Teeth and
They'll Go Away."

Semantodonitics

Rinse used in addition to brushing and flossing can provide added protection.

Over-the-counter fluoride rinses are helpful for children to use once a day with adult supervision.

In the workplace, rather than using toothpaste, have a mouth rinse to brush with. Pour rinse over your brush; this prevents toothpaste dropping in the sink and leaves a pleasant odor.

If there is a problem of tissue inside the cheek area of the mouth pulling off, changing brands of rinse or toothpaste may correct it. If not, consult your dentist.

A salt-water rinse with 1/4 teaspoon of salt in six ounces of water is a good rinse to take swelling and soreness out of gums. However, people with high blood pressure should not use a salt-water rinse.

Soda water can be helpful in the reduction of bacteria and elimination of bad breath. This is also good for chemotherapy patients with sores in their mouths from their treatments.

STIMULATORS

Oral water irrigation devices are good to clean around bridges, crowns, and natural teeth. They should be used in addition to regular brushing and flossing.

Oral irrigation is also helpful in cleaning and exercising the gum tissue.

When using these devices, always use warm water. Let it run through the tube for a few minutes to warm it up.

Brush within
15 minutes of eating.

SEALANTS, CROWNS,...

Sealants are barriers that protect decay-prone areas on back teeth from plaque and acid. Ask your dentist or hygienist about sealants to protect permanent molars.

A tooth-colored material known as a composite resin is used in bonding teeth. This provides a simple solution to problems that once would have required the use of extensive techniques such as crowning.

Crowns, or caps, are the same thing, complete coverage of the tooth. They are used when a large part of the tooth is broken, decayed, or to improve appearance.

Implants attach an artificial anchor directly into the jaw. There are three components of an implant: the anchor in the bone, the post, and the artificial tooth. Implants take time and are significantly more expensive than dentures or bridges.

Silver fillings, or amalgams, are used in about 75% of all single tooth fillings.

An acceptance program has been established by the American Dental Association to examine the many dental amalgams on the market.

Veneers are custom made shells for the front of the tooth only. They are made of general acrylic or porcelain and are affixed directly to the tooth.

Dentures

Denture wearers should brush them immediately after eating and then rinse the mouth.

"You don't have to floss
all your teeth, just the ones
you want to keep."
Semantodonitics

Give your gums a rest by periodically removing the dentures to relieve pressure.

Any appliance or partial or broken tooth in dentures that rubs or irritates the tongue or mouth should be checked and corrected.

When cleaning dentures, have the sink half full of water or a towel placed in the sink to minimize changes of breaking if dentures are dropped.

PLAQUE

PLAQUE + SUGAR = ACID.
ACID + SUSCEPTIBLE TEETH = TOOTH DECAY.

Plaque is a sticky substance that forms within twenty-four hours of cleaning your teeth and gums. It forms an acid that slowly eats the supporting bones of the teeth. Dental disease, periodontal disease, and tooth decay are caused by plaque. The American Dental Association has estimated that three out of four people are affected by plaque at sometime in their lives.

PERIODONTAL DISEASE

Today, three out of four people will develop some form of gum disease.

To keep your teeth a lifetime and to have good dental health, you must have healthy gums. Periodontal disease, or pyorrhea, is a major cause of tooth loss. This is a gum disease that is measured by the loss of bone around the teeth, called "pock-ets." The dentist has a periodontal probe for measuring these pockets in millimeters. A distance greater than three indicates a probability of periodontal disease. Dental x-rays are also used to detect this problem.

Flouride water is
a great defender of decay.

Actisite is a fiber impregnated with tetracycline which is used for ten days to treat deep pockets. To help rebuild bond around teeth, the FDA has approved a synthetic bone-like material.

Signs of Gum Disease

- SWOLLEN AND RED GUMS
- TENDERAND/OR PAINFUL GUMS
- BLOOD ON MOUTH, TOOTHBRUSH OR DENTAL FLOSS
- LOOSE TEETH
- BAD BREATH

Having the teeth cleaned every six months is sufficient unless you experience any of the above signs. If so, teeth should be cleaned at least every three months.

Contributing Factors to Gum Disease

- SMOKING OR CHEWING TOBACCO
- POORLY FITTED BRIDGES, MALOCCLUSION (POORLY ALIGNED TEETH), AND DEFECTIVE RESTORATIONS (FILLINGS)
- HABITS, SUCH AS CLENCHING OR GRINDING, THAT PLACE EXCESS BITING FORCES ON TEETH
- INADEQUATE DIET
- EXTREME DIETING TO LOSE WEIGHT
- AIDS OR DIABETES
- MEDICATIONS SUCH AS STEROIDS, SOME

TYPES OF ANTIEPILEPSY DRUGS, CANCER THERAPY DRUGS, AND SOME CALCIUM CHANNEL BLOCKERS

Tobacco use increases
gum disease.

Treatment

Advanced gum disease is treated by removing plaque and hard deposits above the gums during the first treatment. At the second appointment, half the mouth is anesthetized in order to remove deposits under the gum tissue. The rough fibrous tissue is then smoothed gently to let the gums heal. The root area of the tooth is scaled slick to allow the cleaned tissue to adhere to the teeth.

Facts of Gum Disease

Gingivitis is a gum disease that causes red, swollen, tender tissue to bleed on touch.

The percentage of adults who think they will never develop gum disease is 76%.

The percentage of adults who develop gum disease is 75%.

Bacterial plaque causes 95% of gum disease.

The greatest loss of teeth is caused by gum disease.

Decay

Decay can be greatly increased in a short period of time if hard candy, breath mints, and cough drops are kept in the mouth for long periods of time.

Select a sugar-free cough drop if they're to be used over

forty-eight hours.

All soft drinks with sugar are damaging to the enamel of the teeth.

Change your toothbrush
every three months.

Drinking a sugar-laced soft drink slowly rather than quickly increases acid and decay.

Sensitive Teeth

During childhood and adolescence most decay develops in the crowns of teeth. Later, as gums recede as part of aging or as a result of gum problems, the exposed roots of teeth become susceptible to decay and sensitivity.

Dental hypersensitivity, or sensitive teeth, occurs when the root surface of a tooth comes in direct contact with stimuli such as hot, cold, sweet, sour, or touch.

Desensitizing toothpaste can be used for sensitive teeth. Use it as a cream over sensitive areas after brushing. Apply with a Q-tip several times a day to gum abrasions and recessions.

Sugared mints, chewing gum, and sugared cokes cause more gum line decay and increase sensitivity.

Dry Mouth

Since saliva provides a natural defense against tooth decay, the dry mouth condition suffered by millions of people can in-crease tooth decay and gum disease. Saliva lubricates the mouth, washes food away from around the teeth, neutralizes decay-causing acids produced by plaque, and washes bacteria away.

Severe dry mouth due to medical conditions or medications can be alleviated with artificial saliva recommended by the dentist.

Limit use of alcoholic mouthwashes to once a day or use alcohol free rinses.

Teeth for Life with
Daily Care.

Avoid alcohol and caffeine drinks, and drink a lot of water daily.

Chewing gum helps, but if you must chew gum, be sure it is sugar free.

SORES AND ULCERS

Canker sores may be caused by stress in some individuals. Sodium lauryl sulfate, a foaming ingredient in most toothpastes, has been suspected to be a cause of the problem, also.

Too much cinnamon gum and candy consumption can cause red gums, oral ulcers, or a burning sensation in the mouth.

DRY SOCKET

Dry socket occurs when blood does not stay in the socket after a tooth is extracted.

WISDOM TEETH

If wisdom teeth have to be removed, it is best to do so before the age of thirty. This is simply because younger patients heal more easily.

If all the wisdom teeth need to be extracted, it should be done at one time.

After an extraction of wisdom teeth or any other tooth, keep pressure on the area with a gauze pad to stop bleeding. Slight bleeding is normal for up to twenty-four hours.

Avoid sucking through a straw for forty-eight hours, and avoid lifting heavy objects.

Plaque Sticks to Teeth
Like Honey on a Plate.

Stay away from extremely high temperature foods, alcoholic beverages, and alcoholic mouth rinses.

After twelve hours, rinse with a warm salt water to help healing.

TMJ

Chewing gum over long periods and rapid chewing add to the TMJ (temporomandibular joint) Syndrome in the jaw joint. TMJ can also be caused by nail biting and grinding or clenching the teeth.

To eliminate harmful effects of clinching or grinding, wear night guards and bite plates.

Prime candidates for TMJ are violinists, flutists, singers, and cheerleaders.

Self-help for TM J: rest the jaw, check for habits that are causing the problem, eat soft foods, and apply moist heat.

PREGNANCY

Pregnant women have a very special need to maintain good oral hygiene and regular cleaning and checkups. Hormonal changes can cause gingivitis, but the greatest cause of dental problems during pregnancy is nausea. Strong stomach acids cause the teeth to become discolored and cause the gingivitis tissue to become puffy, red, and sore.

This is partly due to not feeling well enough to rinse the mouth or brush and floss care-fully.

Out to eat, No brush &
no floss with you, take
a drink of water after
chewing the last bite of food
and swish and swallow.

During pregnancy, local anesthetics can be used, and if necessary, x-rays can be taken with the use of a lead apron.

New mothers should take their vitamins for four to six weeks after delivery to maintain dental health.

Nursing mothers should still have their regular checkups and cleanings.

Always inform the dentist if you are pregnant or taking prescription drugs.

BABIES

A healthy baby starts with healthy teeth. Dental care should begin right after birth.

A baby washcloth can be used to wipe gums clean. As soon as a tooth appears, use a baby washcloth after feeding to clean the tooth and continue wiping all the gum area.

Baby teeth, or primary teeth, first appear anywhere from six to ten months. These baby teeth reserve space for and guide permanent teeth to proper eruption.

By two years a child should be able to handle a small, soft bristle brush with an adult on hand to assist.

Start flossing a child's teeth when they fit closely together. The American Dental Association recommends that children's teeth should be flossed by three years.

Teething babies can be comforted if allowed to chew on a cold washcloth or a chilled teething ring.

Teaspoon turned over is a
great tongue cleaner.

"Bottle tooth" decay can occur if babies are allowed to go to sleep with a bottle of milk, formula, or fruit juice in their mouths.

A two or three year old still sucking on a bottle will suffer tooth enamel damage.

Bacteria can be transferred from parents to baby by a lot of kissing. It has been found that mothers and fathers with clean teeth start their babies on the road to better dental health.

Six year molars, our most important teeth, appear around the age of six.

Baby molars are present until about twelve years old. It is recommended that children living in non-fluoridated areas use fluoride supplements until then.

Children are very hard on toothbrushes. Check often to see that they are clean and that the bristles are not bent and frayed.

Teach children to play safely. Careless horseplay such as pushing at drinking fountains or running around swimming pools are the main cause of accidental breakage of teeth.

If a child's tooth is knocked out, place the tooth in the socket and get to the dentist immediately. If it cannot be placed in the socket, put the tooth in a container of milk and proceed immediately to the dentist.

If the tooth is permanently lost, a space maintainer may be advised and put in by the dentist.

Orthodontic treatments help in speech and appearance.

Drinking 6 to 8 glasses
of water daily is good
for dental health.

A child's body and teeth need a proper diet for good growth and nutrition. The good news is that the same nutritious foods that reward your body by building strong bones and muscles also help build healthy teeth and gums.

Watching parents brush and floss daily can begin and set good dental habits.

Diet

One of the ways to keep a mouth healthy is to follow a healthy diet. Choose a balanced diet of foods from the four food groups: fruit and vegetables, milk and milk products, whole grain bread and cereals, and lean meat and fish. Drink plenty of water and even pack it in your child's school lunches and snacks.

Good snacks for children are fruits, raw vegetables, cheese, and popcorn.

According to James S. Wefel, Ph.D., a researcher at Dow, cheese, such as cheddar, before a meal can reduce the acid production of plaque.

A good diet for the teeth would be to increase natural foods, decrease refined and processed foods, and keep down intake of sugared drinks.

Sugar gum and soft drinks, especially those with high acid content, cause decay, sensitivity, and mottling (change in color) of tooth enamel. However, chewing sugarless gum immediately after a sugar or a simple carbohydrate snack can help neutralize plaque acids.

Avoid eating cold foods and drinking hot drinks together.

Brush & Floss
before bed.

Eating ice causes the greatest amount of breaking of teeth and fillings.

Eating lemons causes the enamel of the upper front teeth to become thin from the acid, but lemon juice in drinks or other food is not destructive to the teeth.

Avoid between meal snacks, and don't continually or frequently drink, suck, or chew substances that contain sugars and starches.

Eat an apple and rinse with water after meals to clean teeth, and eat parsley to freshen breath.

Heavy tea drinkers have less tooth decay but still need to see the dental hygienist because of heavy stains that form from the tea.

Healthy teeth are a key to a healthy body. A proper diet will ensure that you have both.

Did You Know...?

Teeth can be permanently stained by tetracycline, an antibiotic, if given to children when the primary teeth are forming.

The tetracycline induced stain of permanent teeth occurs between the ages of three to eight.

Very high fevers in children, when the enamel is forming on permanent teeth before they erupt, can cause white spot staining.

People with few teeth and no replacements have greater stomach problems.

Plaque causes 95%
of gum disease.

The risk of cavities and gum disease increases when you eat frequently.

A tooth with a root abscess can be treated with endodontics (root canal) or extraction.

Missing permanent teeth affect other teeth as well as appearance, chewing, and speaking because of gum tissue and bone loss.

Progesterone, found in some birth control pills, can make the gums prone to gingivitis in some individuals.

Inflation has hit the tooth fairy. The average tooth fairy cost is $1 - $2, but in some areas of the United States, the tooth fairy cost can be $2 - $50 per tooth.

YOU SHOULD...

Never let your toothbrush touch another family member's brush while being stored.

Never use another person's toothbrush.

Never put aspirin on tissue around the teeth. It burns off the surface of the tissue.

Brush your tongue to keep bacteria and plaque down in your mouth.

Increase vitamin B intake if corners of the mouth are sore and cracking.

Keep corners of the mouth moistened at night during sleep.

Babies are toothless wonders, adults that are toothless are sad wonders to look upon.

Apply vitamin E to the corners of your mouth to help healing.

Use sunscreen on lips as they have a high susceptibility to cancer.

To keep lips smooth, brush them with a brush softened with hot water.

Rinse mouth with Maalox to help with mouth ulcers.

Use baking soda to clean teeth and to help clear up stains. Use soft toothbrush bristles to better clean gums and teeth. Use a toothbrush accepted by the American Dental Association.

VISITS TO THE DENTIST

Your dental office should have your medical history and should keep it up-to-date.

Home care instructions should be given by your dental hygienist.

Recall notices or a call reminder should be sent by the office.

Patients who are very stressed and fearful of dental work should select a dentist with nitrous oxide. However, you should know that nitrous oxide produces a loss of sensitivity to pain. A local anesthesia can be used with less discomfort.

The new air abrasive unit replacing the high speed drill will help the fearful patient. With this unit, no anesthesia or needle is needed if the cavity is small.

Avoid sticky snack food.

Patients with artificial hips, knee replacements, or a history of Rheumatic Fever should be covered with antibiotics for regular cleanings and all dental work.

Ultrasound cleaners should not be used on patients with pace-makers.

Hygienists should practice barrier protection by using gloves, face masks or shields, eyeglasses, and covering gowns with long sleeves.

Disposable polishing brushes should be used, and all instruments should be steam sterilized in an autoclave.

All buttons, dental lamps, and handles to equipment should be disinfected and covered with new wrap for each patient.

Everyone should have their teeth cleaned every six months. However, those with periodontal disease or heavy calcium formations should have their teeth cleaned every two to three months.

A precautionary note, never eat until the numbness has worn off after a dental visit.

Regular dental checkups are essential for detecting early signs of oral cancer.

ORAL CANCER WARNING SIGNALS

- SWELLING, LUMPS OR GROWTH ANYWHERE IN OR AROUND THE MOUTH.

- WHITE, SCALY PATCHES INSIDE THE MOUTH
- ANY SORE THAT DOES NOT HEAL
- NUMBNESS OR PAIN ANYWHERE IN THE MOUTH

Plaque is a soft, sticky bacterial film that forms on your teeth every 24 hours.

Tartar or calculus, the same, a calcified material which forms on teeth and down the root.

Dental X-rays

Dental x-rays are an important part of the examination of teeth and gums.

The new technology in x-ray, called digital x-ray (digital radiography) is reducing waiting time and radiation exposure.

X-rays help to detect decay, missing teeth, and overcrowding of teeth.

Benefits of X-rays

- FIND CAVITIES WHILE THEY ARE SMALL ·
- FIND PERIODONTAL (GUM) DISEASE THAT CAN CAUSE LOSS OF BONE AROUND TEETH ·
- FIND CERTAIN BONE CANCERS EARLY ·
- DIAGNOSE OVERCROWDING OF TEETH AND MISSING TEETH IN CHILDREN

To stop the "gag" reflex in the dental office when interoral x-rays are taken or impression material is placed in the mouth, raise ankles two inches and hold.

See a dental hygienist
for regular 6 months' cleaning,
or as often as your
dentist recommends.

REMEMBER!

- For good dental health have regular dental checkups and cleanings.

- Fluoride toothpaste is recommended by the American Dental Association.

- Have your teeth maintained in a dental office that has a dental hygienist.

- Any question relating to being a dental consumer can be directed to:

The American Dental Association
Bureau of Public Information
211 East Chicago Avenue
Chicago, IL 60611
(312) 440-2806

A habit takes 21 days to form.

Floss check for you to form the dental floss habit.

1.	11.
2.	12.
3.	13.
4.	14.
5.	15.
6.	16.
7.	17.
8.	18.
9.	19.
10.	20.
	21.

For your dental maintenance record.

Dental Cleaning   Date

Primary Teeth
or
Baby Teeth

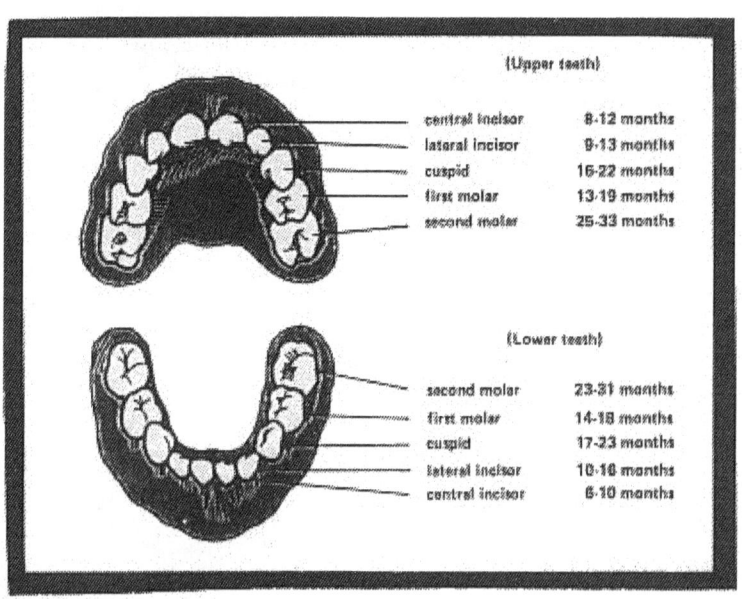

(Upper teeth)

central incisor	8-12 months
lateral incisor	9-13 months
cuspid	16-22 months
first molar	13-19 months
second molar	25-33 months

(Lower teeth)

second molar	23-31 months
first molar	14-18 months
cuspid	17-23 months
lateral incisor	10-16 months
central incisor	6-10 months

America Dental Ass.

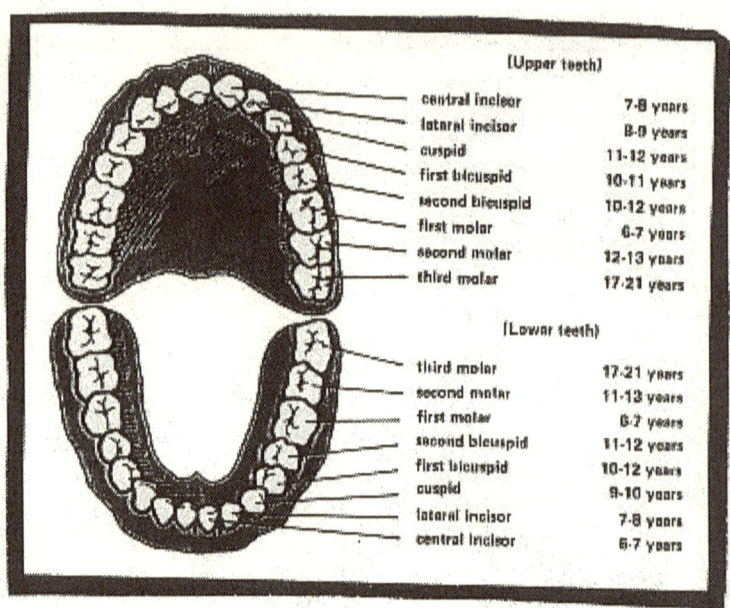

[Upper teeth]

central incisor	7-8 years
lateral incisor	8-9 years
cuspid	11-12 years
first bicuspid	10-11 years
second bicuspid	10-12 years
first molar	6-7 years
second molar	12-13 years
third molar	17-21 years

[Lower teeth]

third molar	17-21 years
second molar	11-13 years
first molar	6-7 years
second bicuspid	11-12 years
first bicuspid	10-12 years
cuspid	9-10 years
lateral incisor	7-8 years
central incisor	6-7 years

Americ Dental Ass.

Notes/Dental Records

Notes/Dental Records

Notes/Dental Records

Notes/Dental Records

Notes/Dental Records

Notes/Dental Records

Notes/Dental Records

Notes/Dental Records

Notes/Dental Records

Notes/Dental Records

Notes/Dental Records

Notes/Dental Records

Notes/Dental Records

Notes/Dental Records

Notes/Dental Records

Notes/Dental Records

About the Author

Dianne Gillentine has been a full-time employed dental hygienist for 32 years, working the last 28 years in the same office. She graduated from the University of Tennessee Dental Hygiene program in 1966 and received the Harold P. Thomas award. She has been an innovator in her small rural area of a given type of home care, to keep your teeth a lifetime.